# FLIGHT

Written by Rob Alcraft

All rights reserved. No part of this work may be reproduced, stored in a retrieval system, or transmitted in any form or by any means electronic, mechanical, photocopying, recording or otherwise, without written permission of Tangerine Press.

Copyright © 2004 Top That! Publishing plc.

Tangerine Press

an imprint of
SCHOLASTIC
www.scholastic.com

Scholastic and Tangerine Press and associated logos are trademarks of Scholastic Inc.
Published by Tangerine Press, an imprint of Scholastic Inc., 557 Broadway, New York, NY 10012
0-439-68103-0
Printed and bound in China

# 24 Contents

| | |
|---|---|
| Introduction | 3 |
| The Dream of Flight | 4 |
| Into the Air | 6 |
| How Things Fly | 8 |
| Staying in the Air | 10 |
| Amazing Aircraft | 12 |
| Amazing Feats | 14 |
| Passenger Aircraft | 16 |
| Combat Aircraft | 20 |
| Jet Power | 24 |
| Supersonic Flight | 26 |
| Vertical Takeoff and Landing | 28 |
| Fly-by-Wire | 30 |
| Gliders | 32 |
| Ultralights | 34 |
| Helicopters and Gyrocopters | 36 |
| Hang gliding | 38 |
| Paragliding and Paramotoring | 40 |
| The Space Shuttle | 42 |
| Future of Flight | 44 |
| Glossary | 46 |

For thousands of years, humans only dreamed of flying. However, this did not stop people from trying to fly. People would jump from cliffs and towers with little more than boards or feathers strapped to them.

### Powered Flight

In 1903, the Wright Brothers made the first powered flight at Kitty Hawk, North Carolina. Orville flew for just twelve seconds. Aircraft developed quickly and soon were flying from New York to Los Angeles, and crossing the Atlantic.

### Modern Aircraft

Today there are aircraft that fly to the edge of space, and others that carry 360 tons of cargo. There are airplanes that transport hundreds of people across thousands of miles everyday. Journeys that once took months, now take hours. Our world seems smaller because of flying. We are connected to more places, and more people, more quickly. Flying is a dream come true.

*Aircraft have come a long way since the first attempts at flight. Today's state-of-the-art aircraft, like this Eurofighter, are far superior to the flimsy wood-and-fabric machines of only 100 years ago.*

# The Dream of Flight

**The first people trying to fly thought they had to copy birds. They built incredible flapping machines or jumped from buildings holding bird wings. Others experimented with kites and gliders.**

### Death Leaps

Nearly a thousand years ago, a man known as the Saracen of Constantinople jumped from a tower wearing a stiff cloak he thought would help him fly. It didn't. In 1874, Vincent De Groof was dropped from a balloon in a flapping ornithopter machine. He plunged to his death. There were many such birdmen. They all failed.

### Model Flight

The first real flying machines were toys. Toy helicopters—propellers on sticks—were made and flown in China and Europe in the 1500s. Then, in 1871, a Frenchman called Pénaud built a model aircraft that actually flew. The model had a propeller powered by a wound rubber band.

### Balloons

In 1783, two men flew five miles across Paris in a balloon. It was the first human flight.

*Belgian shoemaker Vincent de Groof jumped to his death in an attempt to fly.*

# The Dream of Flight

## The First Aviator
Otto Lilienthal of Germany was one of the most important pioneers. He understood gliding, not flapping, was the way to get airborne.

## Dangerous
From 1891, he made over 1,000 flights in gliders he designed and built himself. On August 9th, 1896, Lilienthal crashed flying a new design. He died from his injuries the next day.

## Next Stage
Octave Chanute's glider experiments in Miller Beach, Indiana in 1896 produced the most important glider prior to the Wright brothers.

*Otto Lilienthal glides through the air.*

*An Octave Chanute glider.*

*Even today, birdmen try the impossible!*

**The biggest leap in early aeronautics was the invention of the internal combustion engine in 1885. The new engines were light and powerful. Suddenly, the lumbering weight of steam engines no longer held aircraft firmly on the ground.**

*Orville Wright's plane,* Flyer 1.

### The First Flight

The Wright brothers were the first to build an aircraft that really flew. Their first flight on December 17th, 1903 was a short flight of twelve seconds. Before long they were making flights of more than 30 minutes. The Wright brothers experimented with gliders for years. They understood how to make an aircraft stable, and control it.

### Channel Crossing

Aircraft improved quickly after the Wright brothers showed the world what could be done. In 1909, Louis Blériot succeeded in crossing the English Channel.

### Air War

In World War I, from 1914 to 1918, aircraft were used for spying, fighting, and bombing. Aircraft design improved in strength and speed. The Sopwith Camel flew 105 mph (169 km/h) and could climb to a height of 20,000 feet.

*Louis Blériot lands after crossing the English Channel.*

*A Sopwith Camel.*

huge Short Sarafand flying boat stayed in the air for eleven hours. It didn't need an airport. It landed on water. There weren't many airports in existence at the time.

## Wood to Metal

By the 1930s, the wooden struts and double wings of the early biplanes were no longer used. Now, most aircraft were made of metal. This made them stronger and faster. Some, like the Supermarine S6B, could fly at over 400 mph (644 km/h.)

*The Boeing 247 was the first modern passenger aircraft.*

## Flying Boats

After World War I, the planes people built became larger. The

## Carrying Passengers

Aircraft became the quickest way to travel, and began to carry passengers and cargo. In 1933, the Boeing 247 was the first modern passenger airplane. It had a smooth, all-metal body, and could retract its wheels into the body to reduce drag (the resistance caused by the air).

*The Supermarine S6B could fly over 370 mph.*

**The way a bird's wing moves is very complicated, and requires a lot of muscle control. A human being is not strong enough to fly like a bird. Airplane designers have learned to duplicate the effect of a bird's wing.**

### The Wing

When a wing moves though the air, its shape creates upward lift. This shape—with a curved top surface—is called an airfoil. The lift it creates is the secret of flight. Lift on wings works the same for everything from jumbo jets to paragliders and birds.

*The 1893 Phillips multi-wing, which had many long, straight wings. It never flew.*

### What Wing Shape?

A wing's shape as viewed from above is called its planform. Aircraft have different planform shapes, depending on their speed. Pilots can even alter the planform shape of aircraft with moveable portions of the wings.

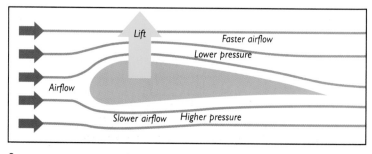

Lift

Faster airflow

Lower pressure

Airflow

Slower airflow    Higher pressure

# How Things Fly

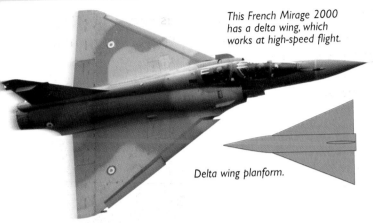

*This French Mirage 2000 has a delta wing, which works at high-speed flight.*

*Delta wing planform.*

## Delta

Delta wings are named after the Greek letter delta, which looks like a triangle. This kind of wing works for high-speed flight, but requires longer runways for takeoff and landing.

## Long and Straight

Long, straight wings work better at low speeds. Gliders and light-powered aircraft have this kind of wing.

*Glider wing planform.*

*Gliders have long, straight wings, which work better at low speeds.*

# Staying in the Air

Bicycles and cars can only turn left or right, but flying is very different. A plane flies in three dimensions. It can go left or right like a car, but it can also go up and down, and tip from side to side. A pilot has to use the following three sets of controls at the same time.

**Yaw**
Pilots can move the rudder pedals with their feet, making the plane go left and right with the rudder on the tail of the plane.

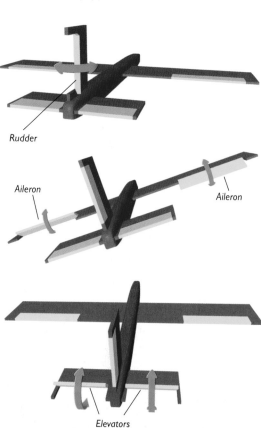

*Rudder*

**Roll**
Moving the control stick or wheel right or left moves the ailerons, which tip the plane's wings one way or the other.

*Aileron*

*Aileron*

**Pitch**
The control stick or wheel moves the elevators. Pushing forward sends the plane down. Pulling it back pulls it up.

*Elevators*

10

## Air Speed

Speed is essential for flight. An aircraft's wings have to move through the air to create lift. If an aircraft goes too slow, it will stall. Different aircraft fly at different speeds. A hang glider can fly at 15 mph (24 km/h), because it is very light. An airliner weighs many tons and will not fly if it goes much slower than 150 mph (240 km/h).

## Drag

As an aircraft flies, it pushes air out of the way. Things that stick out make this difficult —it is like trying to run fast while holding a big flat board in front of you. This is called drag. To help an aircraft fly smooth and fast, designers streamline them to cut down on the drag. This makes the aircraft more efficient.

*Streamlined aircraft like this F-16 fighter have smooth shapes.*

*Formation aerobatic flying requires great skill and precision.*

# Amazing Aircraft

**From the biggest to the fastest, some amazing, unexpected machines have managed to fly—and some haven't.**

### The Widest
At 318 feet (97 m), the 1947 Hercules flying boat has the longest wingspan of any plane. Built entirely from wood, it was nicknamed the Spruce Goose. It flew once.

### One Small Hop
The Wright brothers first flight was 121 feet (37 m).

### Short and Sweet
The Sky Baby is the plane with the world's shortest wingspan—just 5.5 feet (1.6 m).

*The Spruce Goose is now on display in California.*

*The Sky Baby biplane is tiny!*

### Flying Sheep
The first living things to fly in a balloon were a sheep, a chicken, and a duck. They made their flight in 1782. The animals were used as test pilots, to see if there was enough air to breathe high above the ground.

### Bullet Power
In 1870, a Frenchman, Gustave Trouvé, built a flying model ornithopter. It was

powered by bullets! Blank cartridges would fire through tubes, forcing the wings to flap. Amazingly, Trouvé's ornithopter flew over 230 feet (70 m).

## Powered Hops

By the 1890s, inventors across the world were making powered flights. In 1890 France, a steam-powered aircraft with wings like a bat made a short flight.

*The Frost Ornithopter, a machine which flapped, but didn't fly.*

*Clement Ader's "Eole" was another failed ornithopter.*

**Daring has always been a necessary part of flying. Early pilots risked their lives to earn a living and to prove what an aircraft could do.**

### Stunt Women

The 1920s was the age of the flying circus. Pilots and planes toured America and Europe, doing stunts and displays in front of paying crowds. It was women who often did the daring, crazy stunts—including wing walking. There were no nets or safety harnesses. If you fell, you died.

### First Across the Atlantic

In 1919, two pilots, John Alcock and Arthur Brown, made the first non-stop transatlantic flight. Their plane was a converted World War I bomber called a Vickers Vimy.

### Record Breaker

The fastest aircraft in the world is the rocket-powered X-15. It can fly at 4,520 mph (7,274 km/h), more than 300 times the speed of the Wright brothers' first flight and six times the speed of sound.

*Lillian Boyer, a famous "barnstormer" of the 1920s.*

*A Vickers Vimy like this one made the world's first non-stop transatlantic crossing.*

## Faster than a Bullet
The Space Shuttle orbits the earth at 5 miles per second (8 km/s)—more than ten times faster than the speed of a bullet.

## Nose Cone
The Concorde's nose cone grows up to 10 inches (25 cm) longer in supersonic flight. High-speed friction makes its metal body expand—so it gets longer.

## The Lowest Flying Aircraft
Hovercraft are the lowest flying aircraft. They fly on a cushion of air, held in by big rubber skirts.

## Pedal Power
In 1962, the dream of human-powered flight came

*The Gossamer Albatross flew 22 miles (36 km) across the English Channel.*

true. The balsa wood Puffin made the first straight flight over half a mile. In 1979, another pedal-powered aircraft called the Gossamer Albatross flew across the English Channel.

*A modern hovercraft.*

*The world's heaviest aircraft is the Russian-built Antonov An-225. It weighs 600 tons and was built to carry a Russian space shuttle.*

Aircraft carry millions of passengers every year—traveling billions of miles between them. Today air travel is easy, but in the early days it was uncomfortable and dangerous.

### The First Passenger Aircraft

After World War I, there were a lot of aircraft and pilots with nothing to do. In the U.S., a mail service started using old bombers. In Europe, an air service was started between London and Paris. The flight took over 2 1/2 hours and passengers were given hot water bottles to keep them warm.

*The Junkers F-13 first flew in 1919.*

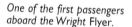

*One of the first passengers aboard the Wright Flyer.*

*Zeppelins were popular in the 1920s.*

*Flying boats could land in exotic, out-of-the-way places.*

### Junkers F-13
The 1919 Junkers F-13 was the world's first purpose-built airliner. It was incredibly reliable, and many planes were still flying after twenty years.

### Giants of the Air
In the 1920s, airships were the luxurious way to travel. The Graf Zeppelins were filled with hydrogen and carried passengers across the Atlantic. The giant *Hindenburg* airship was 800 feet (245 m) long. It would have made a modern jumbo jet look small. Unfortunately, the *Hindenburg* exploded in 1937 over Lakehurst, NJ. Airships lost their popularity after that.

### Flying Boats
Flying boats began intercontinental travel. In the early days, there were only a few airports, but these planes could land in many places. Planes

*A Handley Page 42 in the 1920s.*

like the Latecoere were big. It set the longest sea plane flight record at 3,581 miles (5,763 km) from Morocco to Brazil.

### Handley Page 42
The Handley Page 42 was an old-style airliner that flew 38 passengers in luxury.

It flew over 2 million miles without a fatal crash.

### Dakota
One of the most successful airliners is the Douglas DC-3— or Dakota. It first flew in 1935, and was reliable and quick. Over 10,000 were built, and many are still flying today.

*DC3s are still flying today.*

The age of air travel took off after World War II. The lessons learned from bomber aircraft, and the invention of the jet engine, made fast, smooth air travel possible. The more powerful the jet engines, the bigger the planes.

### Go Large

One of the largest airliners flying today is the Boeing 747, known as a jumbo jet. It weighs over 450 tons and stands more than twice the height of a house. It has a range of 7,670 miles (14,205 km), and has sixteen toilets and six galleys. The 747 is designed for long-haul flying, from one continent to another. The 777-300ER is the largest commercial airliner.

*This French Falcon 900 carries nineteen passengers.*

### Go Small

Not all modern passenger aircraft are huge. Small passenger jets are often owned by companies or rich individuals.

*This Boeing 747 is operated by Australian airline Qantas.*

### Inside an Airliner

Today's airliners have pressurized passenger cabins. Inside the plane, people can breathe recycled air, and stay warm. Outside, the air is very thin and freezing cold. Aircraft built with pressurized cabins can fly above the weather, and give a smooth, comfortable ride. The first passenger planes had to fly through the weather, and air travel was very bumpy.

### The Nuisance of Noise Pollution

Although air travel is very popular, people do not like flight paths to pass over their houses. Nor do they like airports to be built near their homes. The noise pollution can be disruptive, and traffic also builds up in the area as cars travel to and from the airport.

*Some airports are located near residential areas.*

*Modern airliners are comfortable.*

# Combat Aircraft

**When World War I started in 1914, aircraft were used as spy planes. Their job was to monitor troop movements and artillery targets. Aircraft combat started with pilots shooting at each other with hunting rifles, or dropping grenades.**

### First Fighter

The Vicker's Gunbus was the first specialized fighter aircraft, and flew from 1915. A gunner would sit in the front seat, with the pilot behind. It would take the Gunbus half an hour to reach its maximum flying height of 9,000 feet (2,743 m).

*The gunner in this Gunbus sat in the front seat.*

### Deadly Weapon

The Fokker E111 was a single-wing, or monoplane, fighter. It was the first aircraft fitted with interrupter gear, which let the pilot fire forward through the propeller. For about three months in 1915/1916, the E111 was the most deadly aircraft in the sky.

*A German Fokker E111.*

### Strong and Reliable

The SE 5a was a strong and reliable fighter plane, with a forward firing gun. Some were fitted with bomb racks to carry four 25-lb. bombs. After the war, the SE 5a was used as the first skywriting aircraft.

*The Red Baron's famous Fokker Triplane was painted red.*

## Red Baron

The Fokker Triplane had triple wings. It was famous as the plane of Manfred von Richthofen—the Red Baron. He shot down 20 of his 80 kills in a Fokker triplane, before being shot down himself in April 1918.

## Short Careers

World War I fighter pilots flew in open cockpits. High above the ground, the cold, thin air would slow the engines and the pilots' reactions. The conditions often caused machine guns to jam. It was extremely dangerous. At times during the war, the life expectancy of a new pilot was just two months.

*World War I pilots were daring and brave.*

# Combat Aircraft

**Fighter planes have always been the world's fastest and most advanced aircraft. Today's fighters streak across the sky at amazing speeds, and climb almost to the edge of space.**

*20,000 Spitfires were built.*

**First Jet Fighter**
The Messerschmitt Me 262 was one of the first jet fighters. First used in 1944, it had a maximum speed of 541 mph (871 km/h) and could outrun any other fighter in the

**Massive Engine**
During World War II, the Spitfire was very fast. Powered by a massive 1,554 horse power Merlin engine, it could go 357 mph (575 km/h), and could climb 5,000 feet (1,524 m) in 1 minute 36 seconds.

*The Flying Fortress had a crew of 10.*

**Mosquito**
This bomber could fly at 408 mph (657 km/h), faster than any fighter, and still carry bombs.

**Stay and Fight**
The first Flying Fortress bomber

appeared in battle in 1943. Unlike the Mosquito, the B-17 did not try to outrun enemy aircraft, but fight them. It had a crew of ten, including five gunners. It could fly almost 2,000 miles (3,220 km) and carry 3 tons of bombs.

sky. It could also climb to a height of almost 40,000 feet (12,192 m).

*The Mosquito's frame was built entirely of wood.*

## Russian MiGs

MiG jet fighters are one of the most successful. The Russian-built planes first appeared in 1958,

*The MiG 29 carries "smart" weapons that can be guided onto their targets.*

*The Me 262 was the fastest fighter of World War II.*

but have been updated many times since. The MiG 29 is very agile— it can practically stop in mid-air or fly straight up.

## Big Mover

Moving equipment and troops is an important

for modern armies— and aircraft. The C-5 Galaxy transport can carry more than 135,000 pounds (51,000 kg), from tanks to other aircraft, for more than 2,500 miles.

## Fastest

The fastest jet plane is the SR-71 Blackbird. It flies at 2,193 mph (3,529 km/h), over three times the speed of sound. Its weird shape and matt black color are designed to make it invisible to radar. Its main job is to spy on the enemy.

*The SR-71 Blackbird is the world's fastest jet plane.*

*The C5 Galaxy is huge!*

# Jet Power

Jet power changed flying forever, enabling aircraft to fly faster and higher. In fact, weight for weight, a jet is more powerful than any other aircraft engine. One Boeing 747 engine has the same power as 50 cars.

## How Jets Work

A jet's power comes from forcing a blast of burning air and gas back out of the engine. This blast of gas sends it forward—like the way a balloon will go forward if you blow it up and let it go.

*Modern jet engines are complex and large.*

## Inside a Jet Engine

Big forces and temperatures are at work inside a jet engine. Special alloys and ceramics are used to make the engine's casing and moving parts—so they don't melt or break.

## Compression

A jet engine sucks in air and squeezes it through a system of spinning fan blades. At this compression stage, some engines will compress the air 30 times.

## Combustion

Nozzles spray fuel into the engine, which burns at over 2,700°F (1,500°C.) The air and gas in the engine are squeezed.

## Thrust

The burning gas and air roar out of the engine traveling over 1,300 mph (2,090 km/h.) This gives the engine its forward power, called thrust. As the gases rush out, they turn turbine blades, which drive the compressors in the front of the engine.

## Maximum Power

Afterburners are rings of nozzles that spray burning fuel into the jet's exhaust. The burning fuel adds extra thrust—like adding the power of another half engine, but without any more weight. Afterburners get maximum power from a jet. Fighter planes use them in combat, or for short, high-speed takeoffs.

*The afterburners on this jet fighter give it more thrust.*

## The First Jet Engine

The first working jet engine was built in 1937 in an old factory outside Rugby, in England. Its inventor, Frank Whittle, was a test pilot and engineer. His engine worked— but it often caught fire, and leaked fuel. It was four years before it ran well enough to power a jet plane.

## The Turbofan

Most passenger aircraft are fitted with turbofan jet engines. Turbofan engines have a fan in the front. The fan drags air through and around the engine, adding power and saving fuel.

*Turbofan engines have many rows of fan blades.*

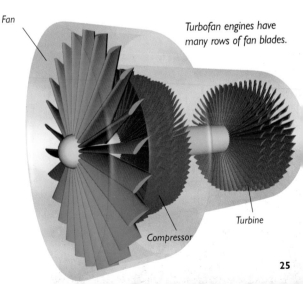

Fan

Compressor

Turbine

# Supersonic Flight

People once believed that flying faster than sound—going supersonic—was impossible. When you think the first flight was only 15 mph (24 km/h), it does seem unlikely. With the invention of the jet engine, planes were quickly flying close to the sound barrier.

### Rocket Planes

The first plane to break the sound barrier was a rocket plane—the 1947 Bell X-1. It was piloted by U. S. Air Force pilot, Chuck Yeager. Rockets work like jet engines, by blasting burning fuel back out of the engine. Unlike jets, rockets carry their own oxygen supply.

The first supersonic plane, the Bell X-1.

### Speedy Travel

The Concorde is the only passenger plane that can fly faster than sound. It cruises over 1,300 mph (2,090 km/h)—and can travel from London to New York in three hours—half the time of a traditional jet. The Concorde also flies over 16 miles (26 km) above the ground— twice the height of ordinary passenger planes. At this height, there isn't much air turbulence, and the Concorde flies faster and smoother.

### G force

When fighter jets turn or accelerate up, gravity pulls hard on the plane and the pilot. This extra pulling force is called G force. Pilots can experience a lot of positive or negative G, and may

Chuck Yeager.

black out because the blood can't pump through their bodies.

**Inflatable Pants**

To help avoid black outs, jet pilots wear an anti-gravitational suit, which has inflatable pads that force blood

*Concorde made its first flight in 1969 and entered commercial service seven years later.*

to the pilot's heart and brain, to stop them from blacking out.

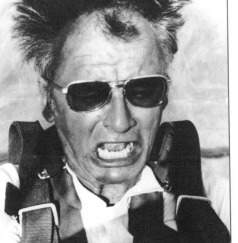

*This aerobatic pilot is showing the effects of negative G force, which forces blood to the head.*

*G suits can help stop pilots from blacking out during sharp turns.*

Not all aircraft need runways to takeoff. Some can take off and land vertically, anywhere, from the deck of a ship to a small patch of grass. These aircraft have some of the advantages of a helicopter, but are as fast as a jet fighter.

### The Flying Bedstead

The first vertical takeoff aircraft was the sensibly named Thrust Measuring Rig, but it looked just a like a bed frame, and everyone called it the Flying Bedstead. It made its first flight in 1954, using four engines pointing down to lift it into the air.

### Up, Up, and Away

Many strange-looking vertical takeoff aircraft were built. The French built the Coleoptére, which flew in 1959. Its giant round body and stumpy wings looked like a comic book

*The French Coleoptére.*

space craft. It crashed two months after its first flight.

### Harrier Jump Jet

Using lessons learned from the Flying Bedstead, the Harrier Jump Jet became the first successful vertical take off and landing aircraft. It made its first flight in 1961— versions of it are still in use today. It uses

*The Flying Bedstead proved that jets could hover.*

*The Harrier is still in use today—more than 40 years since it first flew.*

swiveling nozzles on its engine to give it upward and forward thrust. Once in the air, it can fly 661 mph (1,064 km/h.) It is equipped with missiles, and 25 mm cannons that can fire thousands of shells a minute.

### 21st Century

The Lockheed Martin Aeronautics Company's F-35 Joint Strike Fighter (JSF) will be the world's first supersonic jet fighter with vertical takeoff and landing capabilities.

*The Joint Strike Fighter will be produced in three versions, including this hovering F-35B.*

# Fly-by-Wire

As aircraft become faster, flying them becomes more difficult. Pilot reaction time is one of the main limitations on aircraft design. To help pilots, designers have created a new way of controlling aircraft, called fly-by-wire.

### Out with the Old

Aircraft have been controlled mechanically. That means there's a cable, or hydraulic pipe, connecting the pilot's controls to the control surfaces such as the rudder. It's the same way a bike's brakes or gears are controlled by cables. Fly-by-wire technology gets rid of all the mechanical links and cables, and uses electrical circuits and computers.

### The Electronic Pilot

Fly-by-wire was first tested in the air in 1972 in a U. S. F-8 fighter jet. Fly-by-wire control is not limited by the speed of human reflexes. It enables aircraft—especially fighter jets—to be more responsive and manueverable, because fly-by-wire will keep the wings level where

*Fly-by-wire technology makes modern aircraft more maneuverable, stable and safe.*

*The Joint Strike Fighter would not be able to fly without fly-by-wire technology.*

a human pilot won't be able to.

### High-Speed Help

At high speeds, flying surfaces such as ailerons are forced out of position, and keeping an aircraft stable is very difficult.

Fly-by-wire adjusts the way an aircraft is flying automatically. A pilot can focus elsewhere, like on a target, while the aircraft flies itself. Without the computer, the aircraft would be unstable.

### Idiot Proof

Fly-by-wire technology makes sure a pilot doesn't do the wrong thing, like turn too sharply, or dive too steeply. Some aircraft have a "return to level" button. If a pilot gets in trouble, this function will put the airplane upright and flying safely.

*In the F-16, the pilot moves the controls, and the computer moves the control surfaces.*

# Gliders

**The first aircrafts were gliders. In the 1890s, men like Percy Pilcher made and flew some of the first working gliders. He jumped from hills to get airborne. Today's gliders are hi-tech flying machines made from fiberglass and plastics.**

## Early Gliders

Many people believe that the first successful airplane glider was built in 1853 by Sir George Cayley. He employed his coachman to fly it.

## Super Fliers

Modern gliders are very aerodynamic. Their smooth shape cuts through the air with very little

*Percy Pilcher's 1899 glider.*

resistance. They fly very efficiently, gliding 100 feet (30.4 m), while losing only 2 feet (0.5 m) of altitude.

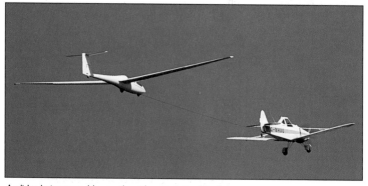

*A glider being towed by another plane to gain altitude.*

*Some gliders have small engines that pilots turn off when they want to glide.*

### Expert

In a glider, you can soar above the ground for hours. The secret is catching thermals, or rising currents of air, the same way surfers catch waves.

### Takeoff

Gliders need help getting into the air. The best way to get a glider airborne is to have a tow from a powered plane with a towline. A glider can get high up in the air before they are on their own to glide back to Earth.

### Solo Flight

Glider pilots need an average of 50 takeoffs and landings with an instructor before they can fly solo.

### Know your Stuff

You can train to fly gliders when you're only sixteen years old, but there's a lot to learn. Pilots need to know how the weather works, how to navigate across open country, and how to fly the glider safely. Student pilots fly slower, more stable machines and in very good weather.

### Airbrakes

Gliders do have brakes. These big flaps open up to slow the glider as it lands.

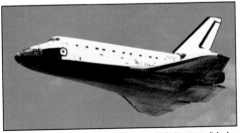

*The Space Shuttle is probably the world's biggest glider!*

**Ultralights are basic flying machines that are easy to fly and take care of. They can take off and land in a field, then fold up and fit on a trailer.**

### Take your Pick

There are two basic types of ultralights, many can carry two people. Some look—and fly—like small airplanes. Others, often called trikes, are like a hang glider with an engine. These trikes have open cockpits which hang underneath the wing.

*Some ultralights look like flying lawn chairs!*

*A flexwing ultralight taking off.*

### Power

The first ultralights were just hang gliders with engines attached. Some even used motorcycle engines. Today they use light, specially built engines. They carry enough fuel for about four hours flying, and cruise at around 30 mph (48 km/h.)

### Launch

Ultralights don't need a lot of runway space. Their takeoff speed is just 20 mph (32 km/h)—you can probably ride your bike that fast! When the machine reaches this speed, the pilot pushes forward on the control frame, and launches into the air.

## Where To?

Ultralight pilots plan their route before they take off, so they know where to land if they have a problem.

## Rules

When ultralights first flew, there were no rules and no training. Anyone could—and did—just build their own ultralight and teach themselves to fly. It was a lot like the early days of flying. This freedom was a big reason why many people took up the

*A flexwing ultralight touching down.*

sport. Unfortunately, some early ultralight pilots crashed and were killed. Today there are strict rules for building and flying

ultralights. You have to be at least seventeen years old before you can get a license to fly an ultralight.

*This three-axis control ultralight has conventional aircraft controls.*

# Helicopters and Gyrocopters

**Helicopter flight was the first flight imagined by humans. Ancient Chinese children played with a hand-spun toy that rose upward when spun.**

### Early Inventor

The Italian painter/inventor, Leonardo da Vinci, made drawings of a machine that looked a lot like a helicopter 500 years ago. His design, like many others, worked in theory, but didn't actually fly. All early models lacked a true understanding of the nature of lift and an adequate engine.

*Modern helicopters are fast and safe.*

### Problems Solved

Once the internal combustion engine was developed, it provided a suitable power source. Engineers had to experiment with an engine that had a rotor to force the fuselage to rotate in the opposite direction to the engine.

### Off the Ground

On November 13th, 1907, a French man named Paul Cornu lifted a twin-rotored helicopter into the air (entirely without assistance from the ground) for a few seconds. This was probably the world's first helicopter flight.

*Leonardo da Vinci envisioned the helicopter hundreds of years ago.*

# Helicopters and Gyrocopters

## Invaluable

Nowadays, helicopters are one of the most versatile and important vehicles in the world. They are used to transport people to various locations which are difficult to reach with other vehicles, such as oil rigs, aerial photography, delivering mail to remote areas, and for several uses on large farms. They are used by emergency services to transport injured people to a hospital, as search and rescue vehicles, to help extinguish forest fires, to monitor the traffic on busy roads, and to assist in the capture of criminals.

## Military Helicopters

The military use helicopters to carry equipment and troops, as assault aircraft, as gun ships, as antisubmarine aircraft, for electronic warfare, and for humanitarian missions.

*Helicopters can help put out forest fires.*

## No Wings!

Gyrocopters have rotor arms instead of wings. These rotors might look like a helicopter's, but they're not powered by an engine. Instead, they spin as the gyrocopter moves through the air. Each rotor arm is shaped like a wing. As they spin they act like wings, to give the gyrocopter lift.

*A military rescue helicopter.*

*A 1930s Cierva gyrocopter.*

# Hang gliding

**Hang gliding is as close as you can get to soaring like a bird. Pilots have to jump from hills or cliffs to get into the air. Once airborne, hang glider pilots catch wind and rising air that can carry them higher and keep them flying, just like birds.**

### Flying Wings

Hang gliders are simple flying wings. They can be put together in about ten minutes. They are made with tough nylon, stretched over a frame made of aluminum tubes, and held tight by steel wires. They weigh about 60 lbs. (22 kg). The first modern hang gliders were built by NASA, who designed them to land space capsules.

*Hang gliders are made from tough nylon.*

### Getting into the Air

Hang gliders do not have an engine. To get airborne, hang glider pilots use hills and cliffs. They lift the glider and run downhill, into the wind.

### Harness

The pilots hang in a harness that looks like a sleeping bag. This harness has pockets to hold maps and a small two-way radio. Also, it keeps the pilot warm. Pilots carry a variometer which tells how fast they are rising or falling. It is information the pilot needs to tell if he is going up or down.

*Hang glider pilots hang in a harness.*

## Control

To control and steer a hang glider, the pilot uses the weight of his body. For instance, if he pulls on the control bar, and shifts his body forward, the glider will speed up and descend. If he moves his body to the right the glider will turn right.

## Staying in the Air

Once in the air, there are two ways a hang glider can stay flying. One method is to catch thermals, which are currents of warm air rising from the ground. If the hang glider circles in these, it will gain height. The other way is to use

*A pilot uses his body to direct the hang glider.*

ridge lift—where wind coming up against a hill or cliff will hit it and rise. Pilots can fly back and forth along a hill using this rising air to stay aloft. The longest flight lasted 36 hours.

*Soaring with the birds!*

# Paragliding and Paramotoring

**Paragliding is one of the simplest kinds of flying. The paraglider pilot hangs underneath a large flexible wing. If a pilot can catch wind from hills and rising patches of warm air, he can stay flying for hours. The distance record for paragliding is 209 miles (336 km), set in South Africa in 1995.**

### A Paraglider Wing

The paraglider wing is made of tough, lightweight nylon. It has compartments that inflate as air passes through them. This gives the paraglider the shape of a wing and provides lift.

*Paragliding pilots use brakes to control direction.*

*Gliding down a mountain.*

### Jumping off Mountains

Paragliding began when new, steerable parachutes were invented in the 1960s. People had the idea of using them to glide down mountains. The mountains had to be high and steep, so only people living in the Alps could fly the first paragliders.

**Flying boat** An aircraft with floats instead of wheels.

**G force** The force that pulls down on a pilot as they accelerate away from or toward the Earth, or make a sharp turn.

**Galley** The name for a kitchen in a boat or aircraft.

**Glider** An aircraft with no engine.

**Gravity** The pull of the Earth, the force that keeps our feet on the ground.

**Gyrocopter** A propeller-driven aircraft with rotor blades instead of wings.

**Harness** The straps and gear that hold a pilot safely in place.

**Helicopter** An aircraft with a spinning rotor, instead of wings.

**Horsepower** A measurement of an engine's power. Many of today's cars have engines of 100 horse power.

**Internal combustion engine** An engine that burns gas. The burning fuel forces pistons up and down, which turn wheels and gears.

**Interrupter gear** A way of making sure a machine gun does not fire into an aircraft's propeller.

**Jet engine** Works by squeezing and burning gas and air, and forcing these to explode out of the back of the jet engine. This makes forward thrust.

**NASA** National Aeronautics and Space Administration, set up by the American government to experiment with flight and space travel.

**Navigate** Find your way around.

**Orbit** The loop around the Earth traveled by a satellite, space craft, or other object in space.

**Ornithopter** Invented name for early flying machines that had flapping wings.

**Oxygen** A gas that people need to breathe, and make things burn.

**Paraglider** A kind of flying that uses a large wing—like a parachute.

**Pressurized** Air pressure is highest on the ground, and much lower high in the air. An aircraft that is pressurized keeps the same air pressure no matter how high the aircraft goes. This keeps the passengers comfortable.

**Propeller** A spinning blade that can pull or push an aircraft through the air.

**Rocket engine** An engine that works like a jet engine. It squeezes and burns gas, forcing it back out of the engine to create forward thrust. A rocket carries oxygen and does not burn air. Rockets can work in space.

**Rudder** A moving flap on the tail of an aircraft that helps the pilot turn an aircraft left or right.

**Soaring** Gliding high in the air.

**Solo** Flying alone, without an instructor.

**Stall** When a plane flies too slow, it drops quickly into a downward dive.

**Steam engine or steam power** An engine that uses steam to force a piston up and down, and turn wheels and gears.

**Strut** A support or bar added for strength.

**Supersonic** Traveling faster than the speed of sound.

**Thermal** A name for a rising patch of warm air.

**Thrust** A pushing force.

**Turbine** A turbine is a set of spinning blades. Turbines work like a windmill.

**Smart weapon** A name for rockets and missiles that can follow and choose targets.

Key: top - t; middle - m; bottom - b; left - l; right - r;
APL - Aviation Picture Library (www.aviationpictures.com)

Front Cover: (l, r) Corel; (m) Digital Vision. Back Cover: Corel. **1:** Digital Vision. **2/3:** EADS/APL. **4:** Getty Images. **5:** (t) APL; (m) Philip Jarrett; (b) Getty Images. **6:** (t) Getty Images; (b) John Stroud Collection/APL. **7:** (t) Getty Images; (m, b) John Stroud Collection/APL. **8:** (t) Philip Jarrett; (b) TTAT. **9:** (t, b) Corel; (m) TTAT. **10:** TTAT. **11:** Corel. **12:** Austin J. Brown/APL. **13:** (t) Philip Jarrett; (b) APL. **14:** (t) Getty Images; (b) Corel. **15:** (t) Getty Images; (m) Flat Earth; (b) Corel. **16:** (t) APL; (b) Philip Jarrett; (bl) APL/QPL; (br) Getty Images. **17:** (t) John Stroud Collection/APL; (b) Corel. **18:** (t) Francois Robineau-Dassault/APL; (b) Austin J. Brown/APL. **19:** (t) Austin J. Brown/APL; (b) APL/Airbus. **20:** (t) John Stroud Collection/APL; (b) Getty Images. **21:** (t) Corel; (b) Philip Jarrett. **22:** (t) Austin J. Brown/APL; (m,b) **23:** (t, b) Corel; (ml) Getty Images; (mr) Digital Vision. **24:** APL/General Electric. **25:** (t) Corel; (b) TTAT. **26:** Getty Images. **27:** Austin J. Brown/APL; (b) Philip Jarrett. **28:** (t) Philip Jarrett; (b) Getty Images. **29:** (t) Austin J. Brown/APL; (b) Lockheed Martin Aeronautics Company. **30:** Digital Vision. **31:** (t) Lockheed Martin Aeronautics Company; (b) Corel. **32:** (t) Getty Images; (b) Austin J. Brown/APL. **33:** (t) Austin J. Brown/APL; (b) Corel. **34:** (t) Corel; (b) Airsport Photo Library. **35:** (t) Austin J. Brown/APL; (b) Airsport Photo Library. **36:** (t) Philip Jarrett. **37:** (t) Austin J. Brown/APL; (m) Corel; (b) Getty Images. **38:** (t) Austin J. Brown/APL; (b) Airsport Photo Library. **39:** (t) Airsport Photo Library; (b) Corel. **40:** Corel. **41:** (t) Austin J. Brown/APL; (b) Corel. **42:** Corel. **43:** Corel. **44:** (t) EADS/APL; (b) NASA. **45:** (t)Airbus S.A.S.; (b) Austin J. Brown/APL. **46:** Lockheed Martin Aeronautics Company

*Paramotor engines form part of the harness.*

### The First Jump

Paragliders are based on parachutes that are, along with balloons, the oldest way of flying. The first parachute jump was in 1783. A man called Louis Lenormand jumped from a tree, and landed successfully. Modern paragliders are based on the same idea, but are more advanced. Today's paraglider wings weigh only 10 lbs. (4 kg).

### Brake Control

Unlike any other kind of aircraft, paragliders are controlled by brakes. The brakes are two sets of control lines attached to the wing. By pulling on one brake line, the pilot can steer the paraglider left or right.

### Paramotoring

Some paragliders have engines. This is called paramotoring. A paramotoring pilot actually wears the engine with the harness. Engines can weigh 37 lbs. (14 kg). Paragliders can fly around 25 mph (40 km/h) and stay in the air for about two hours.

*Paragliding is based on parachuting.*

# The Space Shuttle

**The space shuttle is part rocket-powered space ship, part glider. It is the world's first aircraft that can fly into space, and return to be used again.**

### A lot of Parts
Each shuttle craft is made from over 600,000 different parts. Over 15,000 people are needed to prepare each shuttle mission for space.

### Countdown
The shuttle's countdown to lift-off is 3 1/2 days long. To check for malfunctions.

### Lift-off
The shuttle's five main engines ignite, and the shuttle rockets out of the atmosphere. Two minutes after lift-off, the shuttle is already 25 miles (41 km) above the Earth.

### Back to Earth
After lift-off the two long booster rockets are empty, so they fall back to Earth to be used again.

*3... 2... 1... lift-off!*

### Fast Escape
The shuttle must reach a speed of 28,000 mph (45,000 km/h) to escape Earth's gravity. After eight minutes, the shuttle leaves the atmosphere and the external fuel tank falls away and burns up on re-entry.

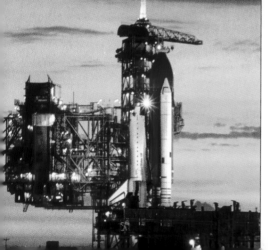

*Preparing for lift-off.*

# The Space Shuttle

*Walking in space.*

## More Parts

Once in space, the shuttle has 44 small rocket engines that help it maneuver. On the flight deck, there are over 2,100 switches!

## Take a Walk

Space walks are part of many missions. Astronauts leave the shuttle in special suits to work outside the craft. The conditions are extreme. The side of the suit facing the Sun may reach 300°F, while the dark side can be around −200°F.

## Coming Home

The shuttle re-enters Earth's atmosphere at 25 times the speed of sound. The friction of air rubbing against the shuttle heats its skin until it glows red hot. To protect the shuttle from the heat, it is covered in 34,000 special heat-resistant tiles.

*Opening the cargo doors.*

*Touchdown!*

## Big Glider

The shuttle glides through Earth's atmosphere. When it lands, the shuttle is going 215 mph (350km/h), and needs 1.5 miles(2.5 km) of runway to stop.

*A parachute helps slow down the shuttle.*

Only 100 years ago, aircraft were flying at just 15 mph (24 km/h.) Planes were built of wood and cloth, and a half-hour flight was amazing. Today, aircraft of 600 tons can heave themselves into the air. If things have changed this much, think what flying will be like in the future!

### Smarter?

The Eurofighter uses the latest computer technology. Pilots are able to choose targets just by looking at them. The plane is programmed to talk—giving pilots warnings and information.

*A vision of the future—the Eurofighter.*

### Higher?

Perhaps space flight will become even easier. The X-33 was one idea for an Earth to space aircraft, but it was too expensive to build. Another idea was the Horizontal Take Off and Landing (HOTOL) aircraft. The HOTOL was to have rocket engines that didn't need heavy tanks of oxygen. However, this aircraft has also proved too expensive to build.

*The X-33 too expensive to build.*

*The A380 will carry 800 people.*

### Bigger?
Passenger aircraft are getting bigger. The Airbus A380 is designed to carry over 800 people Flights like this mean a lot of people can fly a long way at a low cost.

### Smaller?
Bigger is not always better. Some airline companies are betting on small aircraft. These will take people to small airports closer to where they actually want to be.

### Just Different
Aircraft, like the Boeing V-22 Osprey, are flying now. It tilts its propellers and takes off vertically. Then, it rotates its propellers for high speed flight.

*The Boeing V-22 Osprey.*

45

**Aerobatics** Airplane stunts.

**Aerodynamic** A smooth shape that moves easily through the air.

**Ailerons** Moving surfaces on an aircraft's wings. Pilots use the ailerons to roll a plane left or right.

**Air turbulence** Bumps and jumps caused by rising air.

**Airfoil** The special shape of an aircraft wing, curved on top, and flat on the bottom. As it moves through the air it produces upwards lift.

**Airliner** An aircraft built to carry a lot of people.

**Airship** A powered, cigar-shaped balloon that carries passengers.

**Aluminum** A light metal used to make aircraft .

**Biplane** An aircraft with two sets of wings.

**Cargo** A load that needs to be carried.

**Ceramic** Non-metal materials made by firing in a kiln the way clay is made into pottery.

*F-117 Stealth Fighter.*

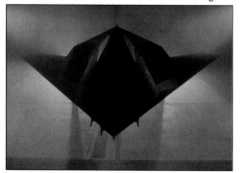

**Cockpit** The place where a pilot sits.

**Composites** Modern materials that are light and strong.

**Control frame** An A-shaped frame on a hang glider or ultralight.

**Control surfaces** An aircraft's moving flaps such as the rudder.

**Design** How something should look and work.

**Drag** The slowing force on an aircraft as it pushes through the air.

**Elevators** The moving surfaces on the stabilizer. A pilot uses the elevators to climb or dive.

**Fiberglass** A strong and easily shaped material, often used in gliders. It is also light.